HANNAH AND DEXTER
LITTER BUSTERS

by

Shiela Martina

Illustrated by Sangi Parvin

MARTINA PUBLISHING, INC

MsLiteracy.com

Martina Publishing, Inc., PO Box 1216, Walterboro, SC 29488
www.MsLiteracy.com

Hannah and Dexter: The Litter Busters
Written by Shiela Martina. Illustrated by Sangi Parvin
Summary: In this third book in the Hannah and Dexter Series, their teacher Ms. Rightover gives an Earth Day project while Hannah and Dexter try to find common ground and gain more knowledge about littering.
(Earth Day is April 22nd every year)

[1. Litter—Environment. 2. Friends—Multicultural.
3. School—Class Assignment. 4. Earth Day—April. I. Title.]

ISBN: 978-1-957645-99-5

Ages 3 - 10

©2022 Printed in the United States of America

Dedicated to

Children who care about the environment!--SK
All the children in the world!--SP

Special Thanks to

Elizabeth Laney, Carolyn Burns, Frances Downing, Cherry Keaise, Nadine Johnson, and Carollyn Lee Peerman

It was a bright and beautiful April morning. The sun beamed gently on the mossy oak trees while Hannah and Dexter made their way to school.

They were glad to be in Ms. Rightover's class again.
When all of her students sat down, Hannah and
Dexter joined in as Ms. Rightover sang her greeting
song to her students before starting class.

Let's start at the very beginning

The class must be quiet to start

When you read, you begin with A-B-C

When you learn, you begin by listening to me! Mmmm.

Ms. Rightover, their 4th grade teacher, welcomed her class and wrote their first project on the Smartboard. Hannah and Dexter were thrilled. They remembered how they won a trip to Washington, D.C., for having the best history project in Ms. Rightover's class.

LOVE YOUR ENVIRONMENT
Earth Day Project
due in
Two Weeks!

Before Ms. Rightover could tell them about the assignment, Hannah raised her hand and asked, "Can we write on any topic we want for the Environment Project?"

"Yes, Hannah, as long as you research ways to improve our community," Ms. Rightover said.

Hannah wiggled in her chair and asked, "Can we partner on this project?"

With a chuckle, Ms. Rightover answered, "Yes, Hannah. The Earth Day project is a group project, and you may choose your partner for the assignment."

Dexter said to Hannah, "Our report will be the best!"

The class went into a buzz of excitement, with each team claiming they would be the best. Hannah and Dexter smiled when they saw Ms. Rightover standing up because they knew she was about to sing. Their teacher sang the requirements for the project to the tune of "He's Got the Whole World in His Hand."

You need to choose a topic and make it good
You need to choose a topic and make it good
You need to choose a topic and make it good
Then present to the class in two weeks.

The class quickly calmed down and started working on their new assignment.

"So, Hannah, what should we focus on to improve our environment?" asked Dexter.

"Well, Dexter, we could focus on littering because there's too much litter around our school," said Hannah.

"You're right. We could call our project Litter Bangers," suggested Dexter.

"I think Cleanup Busters sounds better," said Hannah.

Ms. Rightover overheard Hannah and Dexter having difficulty deciding a topic and said, "I like both of them. So, why not combine your topic ideas and call it the Litter Busters?"

Hannah and Dexter agreed, "Yeah, Litter Busters!"

Later that afternoon, Hannah and Dexter walked to the Colleton County Library to work on their assignment. They saw trash everywhere. They agreed that littering makes the community look bad.

Dexter said, "We need to tell the class how bad it looks when people throw trash around the community."

Hannah added, "We need to tell them to respect the environment because if we respect our land, we will keep it clean."

"When I was coming from school on Monday, I saw trash falling from Mr. Sam's pickup truck on the road," said Dexter.

"This book says that's still littering," commented Hannah.

"Yeah, but I don't think people know that because I see it a lot," said Dexter.

Hannah and Dexter were the first to present their report. They had pictures, posters, and signs.

Hannah said, "We want to tell you how to be Litter Busters like us."

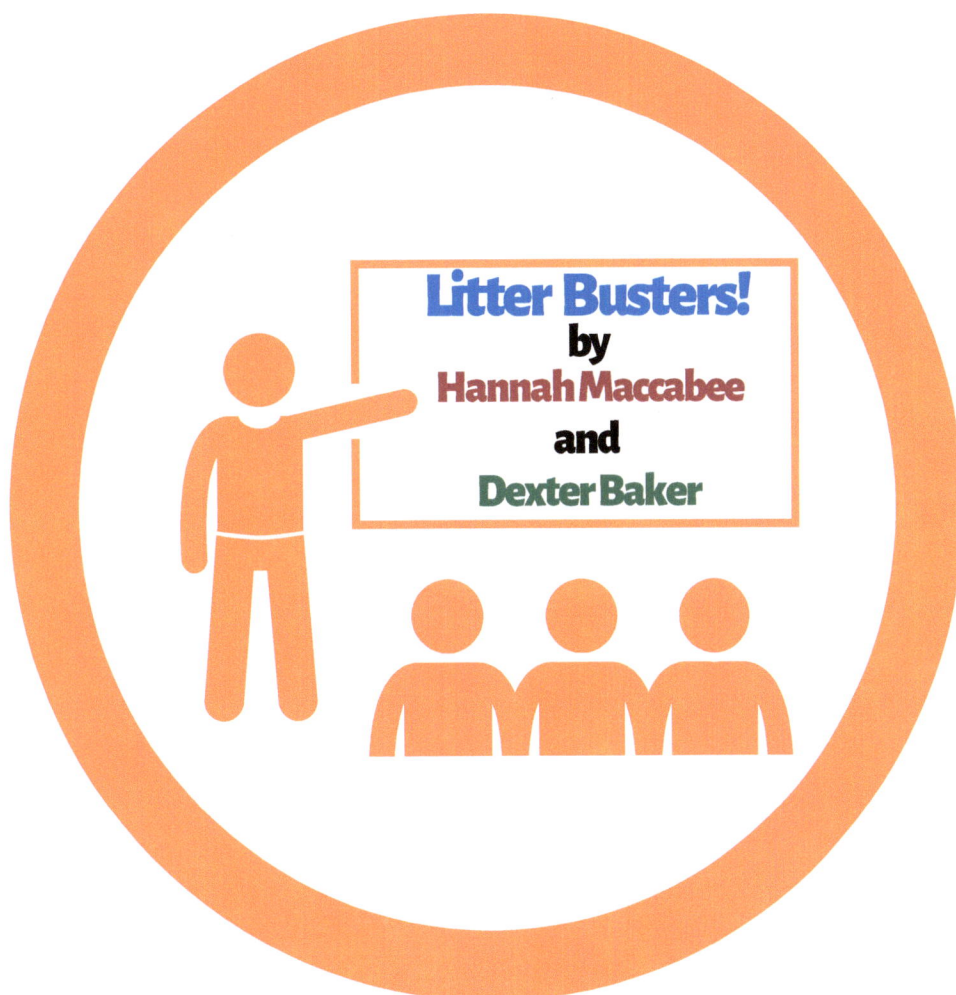

Hannah and Dexter told what they learned by picking up trash at the beach, researching at the library, and observing the neighborhood:

1. When people litter, it can poison lakes, rivers, and oceans.

2. Littering is not cool.

3. The horrible thing about litter is that too much litter can cause fires.

4. When trash falls from trucks or people throw it from cars, this is littering.

5. Plastic waste disables and kills thousands of animals each year.

Earth Day Projects

R-E-S-P-E-C-T

Hannah made an Aretha Franklin impression when she read, "R-E-S-P-E-C-T!"

R - respect our **Rivers**

E - respect our **Environment**

S - respect your **Schools**

P - respect the **People**

E - respect the **Earth**

C - respect the **Climate**

T - respect our **Teachers**

Dexter pointed out. "Littering is not good for people or animals. Don't litter!"

Earth Day Projects

Hannah said, "Litter is trash when it ends up outside a bin or in a landfill. Litter hurts our environment in many ways."

"That's why we should all be Litter Busters to help clean up our surroundings. If we litter our community, it will look terrible, and no one will want to visit," says Dexter.

Earth Day Projects

Be a Litter Buster like Me!

Be a Litter Buster like Me!

They ended their presentation by saying, "We are Litter Busters because we do not litter. Now, you can join us and be Litter Busters too!"

Ms. Rightover beamed with approval. "Thank you, Hannah and Dexter, for a job well done. You are the school's first official Litter Busters! I agree that people who want a beautiful environment will take time and effort to throw their trash away correctly."

Each group presented their projects that Friday. They covered topics from Recycle Rangers and Pollution Crushers to Climate Changers and Harmful Chemicals. Ms. Rightover was pleased with each presentation, but Litter Busters stood out.

Ms. Rightover said, "Tomorrow morning, we are going to Pinckney Park to pick up trash. Who wants to meet me at 9:00 am to be a Litter Buster?"

She was pleased when the entire class raised their hands. Then, she dismissed her students with this song,

So long, farewell, study hard tonight.
Don't Litter, be clean.
Keep your city bright.
Goodbye, goodbye, goodbye!

The End!

Pinckney Park

THE LITTER ON THE GROUND

(tune of "The Wheels on the Bus")
By Shiela Martina ©2022

The litter on the ground makes me so sad, me so sad, me so sad,
The litter on the ground makes me so sad, so please don't throw it down.

The litter on the ground makes the city dull, city dull, city dull,
The litter on the ground makes the city dull, so please don't throw it down.

The litter in the river hurts the fish, hurts the fish, hurts the fish,
The litter in the river hurts the fish, so please don't throw it down.

The litter on the road makes driving hard, driving hard, driving hard,
The litter on the road makes driving hard, so please don't throw it down.

The litter in the school may cause disease, cause disease, cause disease,
The litter in the school may cause disease, so please don't throw it down.

The litter in the sea kills the animals, animals, animals,
The litter in the sea kills the animals, so please don't throw it down.

The litter in the woods harms wildlife, wildlife, wildlife
The litter in the woods harms wildlife, so please don't throw it down.

Dear children of the world, please pick up trash, pick up trash, pick up trash,
Dear children of the world, please pick up trash, and please don't throw it down.

Now, let's be Litter Buster! (talk and point)

Ms. Literacy
reads
and
sings

Do you help keep your community clean? See if you can answer these questions correctly. If you do, then you are a true Litter Buster and you deserve the button in the next page!

TRUE OR FALSE

1. Litter is trash when it ends up outside a bin or landfill.
2. Half or 50% of littered items are cigarette butts.
3. The least common object found during litter clean-up is fast food litter.
4. It is not essential to recycle trash that we throw away.
5. Women litter more than men.
6. Bangladesh was the first country to ban single-use plastic.
7. Young people and young professionals are the smallest amounts of litter groups.
8. Animals die because of litter in the ocean.
9. Litter will always be with us, and there is no way to end it.
10. If trash falls from my truck by mistake, that is not littering.

Answers to the True/False Statements

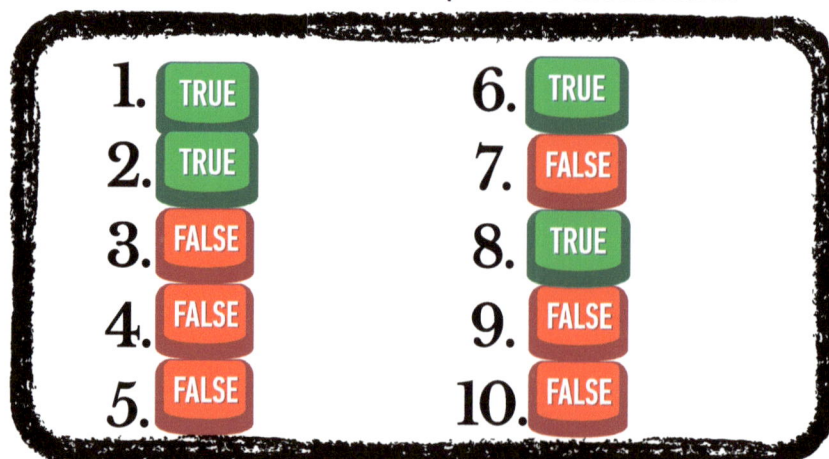

1.	TRUE	6.	TRUE
2.	TRUE	7.	FALSE
3.	FALSE	8.	TRUE
4.	FALSE	9.	FALSE
5.	FALSE	10.	FALSE

Did you earn this badge?
Join Hannah and Dexter and become Litter Busters, too!

My name is

_____

and

I AM A LITTER BUSTER!

ABOUT THE AUTHORS

Shiela Martina is the author of children's and adult books.
She has 25+ years of experience as a children's librarian.
In Shiela's free time, she enjoys singing in church, editing and publishing books for new authors, and taking care of her Aunt's goats, chickens, and cat Bashful.

ABOUT THE ILLUSTRATOR

Sangi Parvin is a professional artist, book designer, creative educator, thinker, motivator, dreamer, and children's book illustrator expert.
She has seven years of experience in this field and lives in Bangladesh, Satkhira, with her father and mother!
She is one of the top 100 most powerful girls on google; everyone finds her there! Her life is not easy, so she wants to work for the kids forever!

www.ingramcontent.com/pod-product-compliance
Lightning Source LLC
Chambersburg PA
CBHW060849270326
41934CB00002B/62